RESOURCE MATERIAL
for
THE EFFECTIVE BOOKSTALL

© Jay books 1990

30 The Boundary, Langton Green, Tunbridge Wells, Kent TN3 0YB, England

British Library Cataloguing in Publication Data
Resource material for the effective bookstall.
  1. Churches. Bookstalls. Management
  I. Thorn, Eric A. (Eric Arnold), *1948-*. Effective bookstall
  381.45002

ISBN 1-870404-08-4

CONTENTS

Jay books

INTRODUCTION

No bookstall can ever be really effective without effective display of its stock allied to well designed publicity. This collection of resource material, used regularly and imaginatively will not only help your bookstall or school bookshop to become more effective, but will also help to project a better image of your enterprise.

Everything in this book has intentionally been kept simple but practicable. The new bookstall, starting from scratch, may utilize to the full such items as card book stands and easy-to-make display models. On the other hand, the more experienced operator will be able to develop more sophisticated designs.

The ready-made artwork is easy to use. Simply cut out the item required and paste it on to a plain sheet of paper. Add your essential information using either a black felt tip pen or rub down lettering, or even typewriting, and you have your "camera-ready" copy! All of the artwork included may be adapted to suit your individual requirements.

If you have access to an enlarging photocopier, you can reproduce the artwork to the size you require, or copy it onto coloured paper.

With special reference to the ready-prepared items of paperwork (invoices, orders, etc), please don't forget to request your printer to insert YOUR details! Wordings given here are intended as guiding examples only!

This book is intended for use in conjunction with THE EFFECTIVE BOOKSTALL, the comprehensive reference book for all those involved with bookstalls, school bookshops, etc.

DISPLAY AIDS

Here are four ideas to enhance your displays.

BOOKWORM

The body consists of cardboard tubes. For a small bookworm, use the centre tubes from toilet rolls. For larger bookworms, use the centre tubes from kitchen towel rolls.

Cover the tube with gift-wrap paper, or decorate it using felt tip pens or poster paints.

Plug the front of the tube with a large ball of cotton wool. To this, glue on small coloured paper shapes for the eyes, nose and mouth. For the antennae, bend a pipe cleaner into a V shape, and insert this into the top of the cotton wool head.

For fringed feet, cut suitable lengths of coloured card with pinking shears, and glue them on to the body. Alternatively, use two strips of "cutters" from clingfilm or aluminium foil boxes.

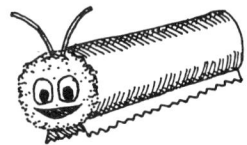

WINDOW EFFECTS

These are suitable for bookstalls or school bookshops situated near a window.

Take a sheet of tissue paper slightly smaller than the size of your window pane. It may be necessary to use more than one sheet, in which case the sheets should be joined with cellulose tape. Fold the sheet in half; then fold in half again; then again.

Cut out pieces from the folded paper to make a pattern to reflect either the season (e.g. leafy pattern for autumn or snowflakes for winter) or your promotion (e.g. stained glass window design to help promote books about cathedrals).

Open out the paper. It may need pressing overnight to get rid of the fold marks. Use tiny dabs of Blutak to fix your paper to the window pane.

With practice, it is possible to produce some excellent effects!

Tree Display

This is particularly useful for seasonal displays.

Three-quarters fill a *small* cream or yoghourt carton (such cartons may easily be trimmed with scissors, if necessary) with filling plaster, such as Polyfilla, and insert a large fir cone.

Leave for at least 48 hours to enable the filler to dry thoroughly, then paint and decorate the fir cone tree as required. An interesting effect is obtained by lightly coating the fir cone with glue or paste, then sprinkling coloured glitter powder over it. Cover the pot with crêpe paper.

For Christmas, a star cut out of card may be glued to the top of the tree.

Egg Display

This is recommended for Easter displays.

SMALL EGGS: Use empty shells from boiled eggs. Place the shells into egg cups, with the open end pointing upwards. Gently fill each shell with filling plaster, such as Polyfilla.

Leave for at least 48 hours to enable the filler to dry thoroughly. Use sanding paper to rub down the open end until the plaster is flat enough to enable the egg to stand up.

Paint or decorate the shell as required.

LARGE EGGS: Blow up rubber balloons to the size(s) required. Cover each balloon with a reasonable thickness of papier maché.

Leave for at least 36 hours to enable the papier maché to dry thoroughly, then paint and decorate as required.

By using a sharp knife, it is possible to trim one end flat to enable the egg to be free-standing.

Another variation is to carefully cut the egg length-ways to obtain two half eggs. Items (e.g. a toy Easter chick) may then be placed into the "hatching" egg.

Mobile

...out round outline. Fold along four vertical ...s. Before gluing, pierce square at top, pass ...ead through and tie a knot inside. Suspend ...ve bookstall.

...ple mobiles with various number of sides and ...arious sizes can be made similarly.

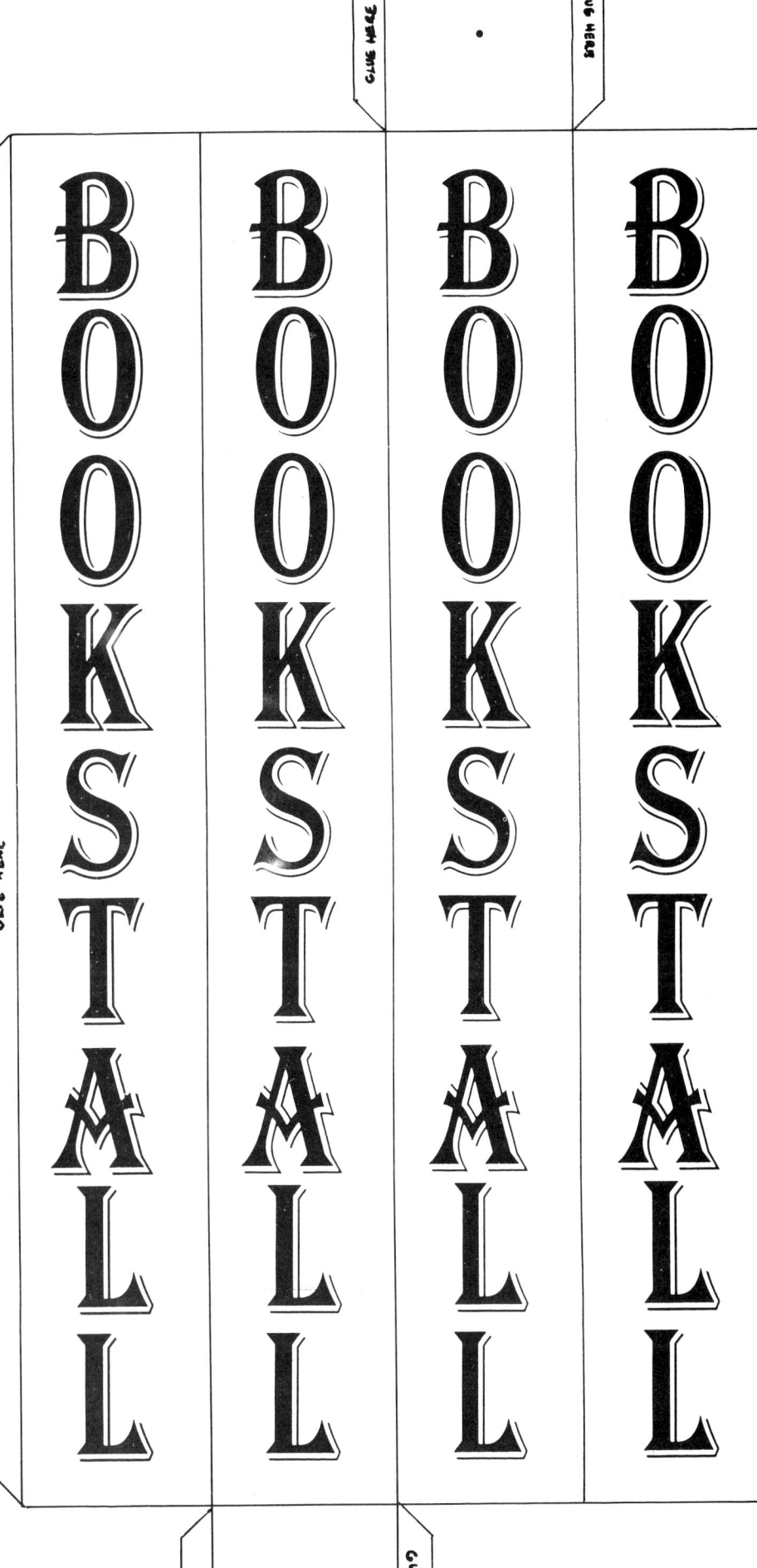

BOOK STAND

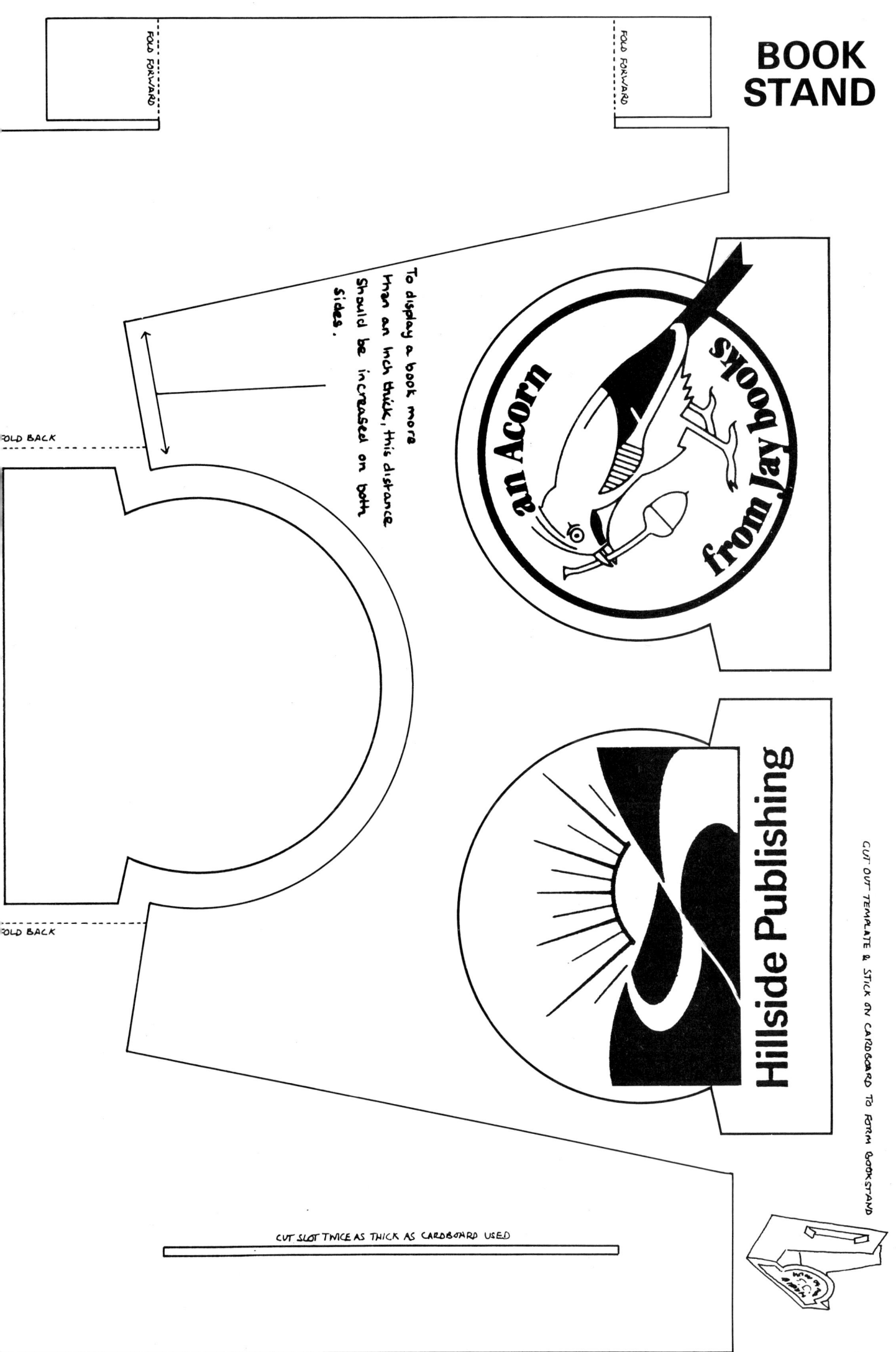

FOLD FORWARD

FOLD FORWARD

FOLD BACK

FOLD BACK

To display a book more than an inch thick, this distance should be increased on both sides.

an Acorn

from Jaybooks

Hillside Publishing

CUT OUT TEMPLATE & STICK ON CARDBOARD TO FORM BOOKSTAND

CUT SLOT TWICE AS THICK AS CARDBOARD USED

Just Published

MAIN

Highly Recommended

National Curriculum

BOOK OF THE WEEK

BOOK OF THE MONTH

BOOKMARKS

add appropriate label and insert into book.

NATIONAL CURRICULUM

RECOMMENDED

BIOGRAPHY

HELP IN STRESS

PRAYER

BIBLE STUDY

RELATIONSHIPS

NEW BOOK

BEST SELLER

THIS IS YOUR

BOOK STALL

USE IT

IF YOU CAN'T SEE IT WE CAN ORDER

ORDERS TAKEN HERE

AVAILABLE ONLY WHILE STOCKS LAST

The dimensions of the labels on these three pages match the cut out stand on the previous page. They can be similarly enlarged as required in a photocopier.

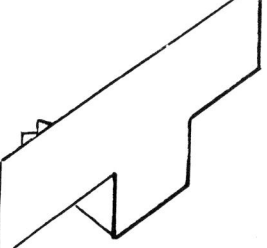

National Curriculum

REVISION NOTES

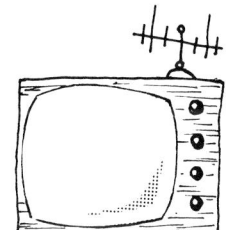

TURN IT OFF! READ A BOOK

STUDY MATERIAL

STOCKTAKING SALE

SECONDHAND BOOKS

 ## NO SECONDHAND TITLE ABOVE 50 P

DAMAGED & SHOPSOILED STOCK

Books for  CHRISTMAS PRESENTS

WE ARE OPEN
FOR BUSINESS

FROM: TO:

1 2 3 4 5 6 7 8 9 10 11 12
:00 :00 :15 :15 :30 :30 :45 :45

Get Reading !

Get Reading !

Book Tokens

Materials

Bookfair

ORDER FORM

Name_____

Address_____

_____

_____

Postcode_____ Tel:_____

Children's Books

Children's Books

Recently Published . . .

MAIL ORDER

MAIL ORDER

Refreshments

Admission FREE

Workshop

CHILDREN'S BOOKS

Christmas shopping

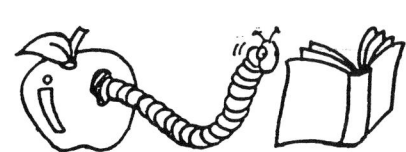

REVIEWS

BOOKS

Invitation

Guest Speaker

LIBRARY

Join Us!

NEWS FLASH!

See You There!

N E W S

REMINDER

LITERATURE

SeminaR

BOOK REVIEWS

JUST ARRIVED

Book Reviews

REVIEWS

Update

Book Reviews

COMMENT

ADMIT ONE

Banquet

Time _____

Place _____

Date _____

BOOK EVENING

Book $^{of}_{the}$ Month

Conference

Competition

COMPETITION

◇ Coffee Hour ◇

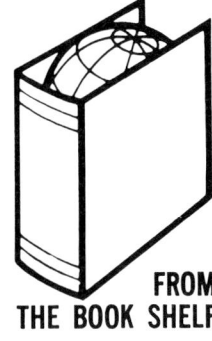

**CASH
SALES
ONLY**

FROM
THE BOOK SHELF

Are your governors allowing enough for books?

L**ITERATURE**
C**ORNER**

Are your governors allowing enough for books?

CHILDREN'S BOOK WEEK

BOOK PRIZES

Book Prizes

LUNCHEON
BOOKS
Dinner *Dinner*
LUNCHEON

ADMISSION FREE Everybody welcome

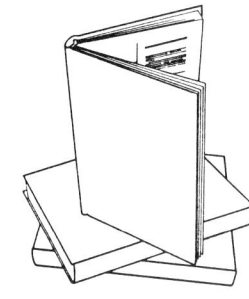

Sale
PAPERBACKS

New Books

BOOK REVIEW

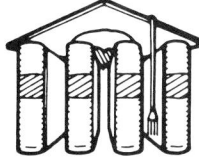

SCHOOL NEWS

RESPECT COPYRIGHT

ENCOURAGE CREATIVITY

Sale Price

BOOK FESTIVAL

VOLUNTARY SERVICE SIGN-UP SHEET

NEED Helpers to assist with the school bookshop at lunchtimes

Your Name	Days Available
1	
2	
3	
4	
5	
6	
7	
8	
9	
10	
11	
12	
13	
14	
15	

Helpers to assist with the bookstall on a regular basis

Alternative Heading:
This may be pasted over lines at top of form before photocopying.

DUTY ROTA

SUNDAY	MONDAY	TUESDAY	WEDNESDAY	THURSDAY	FRIDAY	SATURDAY

Enter in each box the name(s) of volunteers and the times they have agreed to be in attendance.

STATIONERY

The next five pages contain stationery for ordering, invoicing or keeping records. You may wish to add your bookstall or bookshop name and address or other information before you photocopy them or hand them to your printer.

BOOKSTALL INVOICE   INVOICE NO:

To: _____

_____   Date: _____

Quantity	Description	Price Each		Total	
			TOTAL DUE:		

Cheques etc payable to _____

Please refer any queries to _____

Remittance Slip

Please return this part with your payment, thank you

From: _____

To:

I enclose £_____ in payment of your invoice dated _____

Signature _____

TO BOOKSTALL MANAGER: ORDER FORM

Please order the following books for me. I will pay for them as soon as I receive them.

Name: _____ Tel: _____

Address: _____

Qty	Author	Title	Publisher

Paperback   **Hardback**

Please note that all books ordered are kept for two months before being returned to the shelf.

Cheques should be made payable to: _____

Date Ordered: _____

Date Collected: _____ Price: _____

TO

FROM

PURCHASE ORDER

Quantity	Description	Price

ORDER No	DATE	SIGNATURE

Stock Record

Title:

Date	Transaction	In	Out	Stock

PAYMENTS

MONTH: _____ YEAR: _____

Date	Payee	Stock		Expenses		Other		Total Amount	
Total Payments this month									

RECEIPTS

MONTH: _____ YEAR: _____

Date	Customer's Name	Books		Tapes		Journals		Misc		Total Amount	
Total Receipts this month											

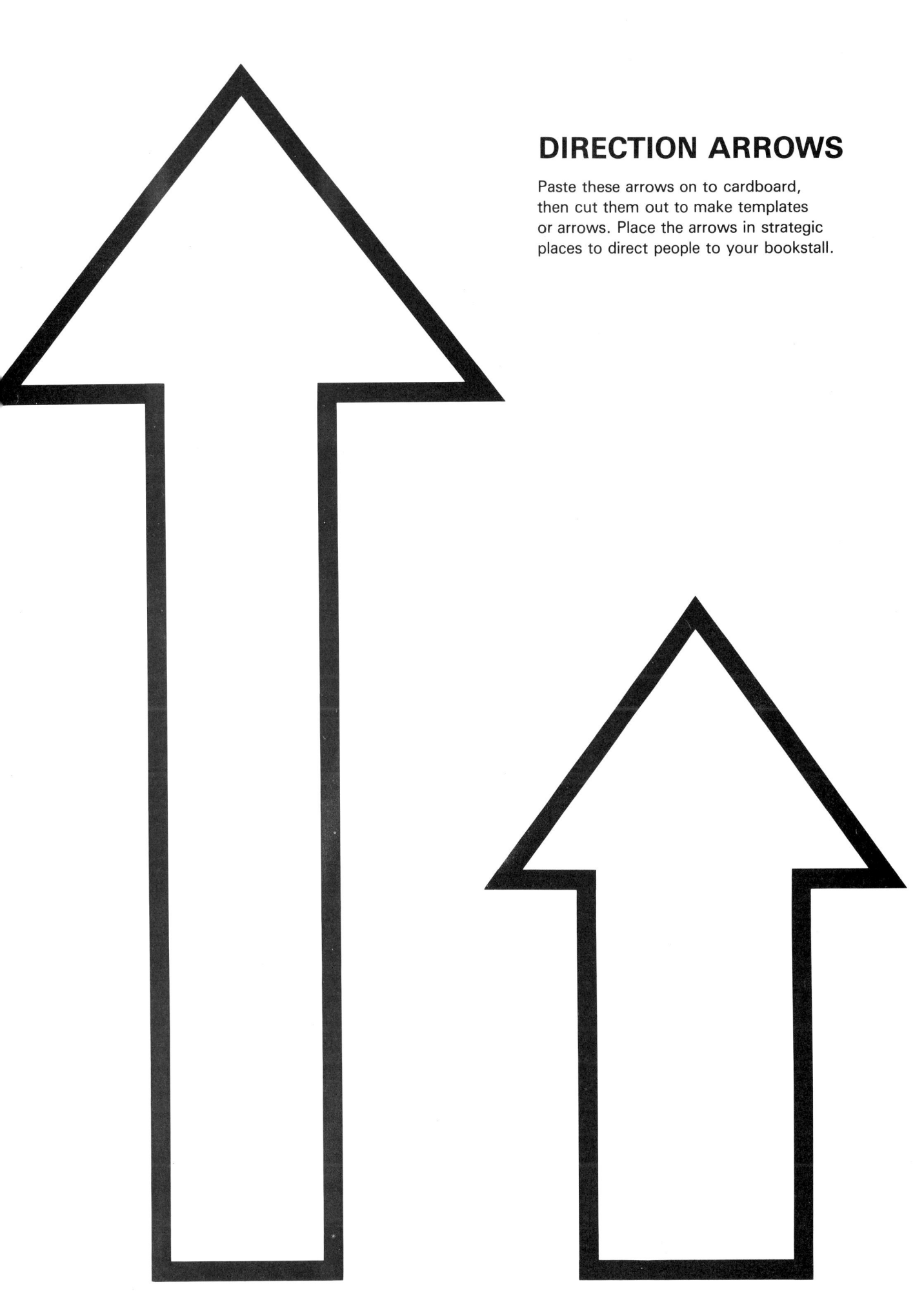

DIRECTION ARROWS

Paste these arrows on to cardboard, then cut them out to make templates or arrows. Place the arrows in strategic places to direct people to your bookstall.

CHURCH BOOKSTALLS?

Use STAX from PointEight

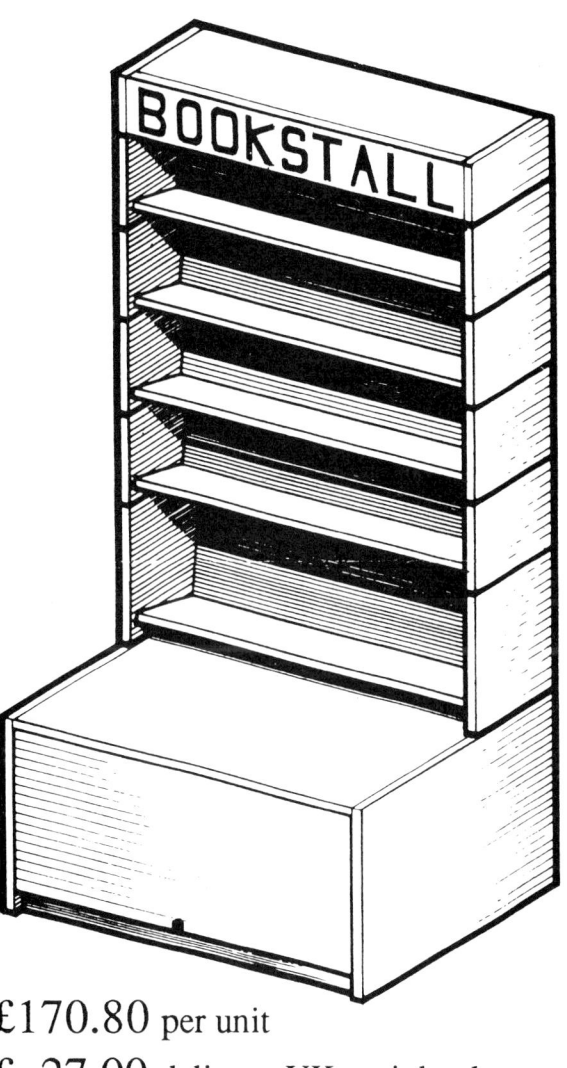

Using components from our very successful Stax range we are proud to offer you a lockable Church Bookstall in high quality maintenance free light oak finish.

Consisting of:

        a lockable base storage unit
        one row of magazines
        and four rows of paperback shelves

the units come complete with a standard "Bookstall" heading or with any title of your choice to order.

STAX stacks! Its that simple.

One shelf stacks on another to build exactly the unit you require. Hardbacks, paperbacks, magazines;

Features:

    * No tools required
    * Easy to transport
    * Simple to put together and take down
    * Interchangeable components
    * Sturdy, durable and attractive

£170.80 per unit
£ 27.00 delivery UK mainland
£ 29.67 VAT

£227.47

Sizes:

Height   2101mm
Width   1000mm
Depth   600mm

Although the above are standard units,
you can design your own from combinations of components from our Stax range.
For information please contact:
POINT EIGHT LTD.
Shaw Road, DUDLEY, West Midlands DY2 8TP
Telephone: (0384) 238282/3/4
Fax: 0384 455746

On the frontline of Christian bookselling?

.. Make sure we're on your kit list!

European Christian Bookseller Review
the monthly magazine for people like you . . . .

Stay in touch with:

- New product info
- Latest news
- Ideas on how to run your bookstall
- Advice on what to stock, what to recommend
- Background on authors
- A place to share your ideas and concerns

Subscribe Today!

Only £18 a year
(12 issues)
– that's only 35p per week!

EUROPEAN
Christian Bookseller
R E V I E W

FREEPOST 144 DEANSGATE MANCHESTER M3 8BB

P.S. Send for FREE issue or phone this number 061-835 3000 NOW!

INVESTING IN A DRUG FREE FUTURE

* Since 1847 the Band of Hope movement has existed to inform and educate people about the dangers of substance abuse.

* Totally committed to playing a relevant part in tackling the present drugs crisis.

* A vital resource base of expertise, materials and personnel for Community, Church and Youth Leaders in the 1990's.

* High quality publications for use with children and young people.

* Conferences, exhibitions and youth holidays.

* Specialist presentations and training in drug-use prevention strategies and programmes.

Concerned for children and youth, the Band of Hope enables families and individuals to educate themselves and make healthy choices regarding the dangers of alcohol and other drug use. As a Christian charity with a proven record of service within the statutory and voluntary sectors, the Band of Hope is available to everyone regardless of belief, race or background.

Millions have met with a drug-related problem. They include innocent bystanders and their families whose homes have been vandalised and belongings stolen; those who have been maimed by drunken drivers; and those who have been terrorised by 'lager louts' or football hooligans. Alcohol is related to 25,000 premature deaths and tobacco to 100,000 each year.

(Royal College of Psychiatrists and Health Education Authority)

* 20% had experimented with drugs.

* There is a rising trend of solvent abuse and smoking amongst girls.

* 45% of 11-year olds had drunk alcohol.

* Teenage users of hard drugs started on alcohol at an average of 10.5 years.

(British Journal of Addiction, August 1988)

JUST RELEASED 'ROY CASTLE' VIDEO

Send today for your FREE Band of Hope Resources Pack

UK Band of Hope, **FREEPOST**, London SE1 0YT

Happy Healthy Drug Free Living Happy Healthy Drug Free Living Happy Healthy Drug Free Living